TORRID *blue*
THE UNDERCURRENT

by Turquoise C.A. Hayes

This book is a journal of the author's thoughts,
life experiences and feelings in poetic expression.

No part of this book may be reproduced, stored in a retrieval system, or
transmitted by any means with out the written permission of the publisher.

© 2007 Christine A. Hayes | Turquoise C.A. Hayes
All rights reserved.

Cover art, graphic design and published by
Christine A. Hayes | Gaithersburg, MD
Washington D.C.

Printed in the United States of America
Washington, D.C.

ISBN 978-0-6151-8381-7

Life Senses

I often hear with my eyes
though I am blessed to hear sounds
reading thoughts and
interpreting scenes
the voice of a painting
the buzz of hummingbird wings
the crack of a bat in a photograph
as faces scream and
hands call out

I often see with my ears
though I am blessed with sight of mind
visualizing sounds and
watching rhythms
the rumble of a bag of chips
the soft hum of a bumble bee
the mischief making of a too quiet child
as the earth sings and
the skies cry

I often taste through my nose
though I am blessed to smell the aromas
drinking fragrances and
consuming odors
the tang of fish frying
the bouquet of vintage wine
the flavor of fresh baked cookies
as perfumes seek and
memories surface

I often breathe with my heart
Though I am blessed to respire with ease
inhaling emotions
perceiving pain
the air of love
the winds of change
the gasp released when witnessing danger
as hope blooms and
atmospheres alter

I often take in this life with acute senses
realizing the blessings that each day holds

By the Tracks

The scent of wet grass,
azaleas, and dandelions
fill the breeze of hot southern air
that gently blows and puffs my curtains
I can hear the call of a train chanting
"it's seven o'clock" through my window

The wheels slide on silvery rails
The same tracks we cross
going to and fro on any route

You're unfamiliar with the song
of the train's whistle
or the rocking of its cars
lest you stay in the bottom
around these parts

Some thought that humming
would be a burden
rapping windows and disturbing dreams
so they laid tracks in low lands
far away from the fancy parts of town

Yet, I found comfort in the train's calling
passing by with traveling tunes
I'd memorize times and count the adventures
each train lent as it carried along

The same trains
now, leave my son in awe
The whistles are young songs
The cars carry renewed joys
and visits from the past
that tarry by the tracks

The Wishing Well

A coin dropped
a heart stopped
eyes released rushing tears
that raced the coin
to waters, still
a pool of emotions
hopes and dreams
joyous or desolate

none sadder than
the wish flung
hopelessly down
this old and crumbling well
surrounded by a dark forest
trees swayed
leaves let in little light
to brighten the mood
of a pale and sunken face

with nervous hands
and shouting mind
she tried to discern
How could this be?
How could she have lost?
Why not she?

The reflection of trees
bowed and hazed
as she replayed
the devastating hour
frame by grueling frame
how one life was ripped
from the arms of another
with crashing force
that severed ties and limbs

Blood drenched and stained
she ran through wooded land
where she had often visited
as an unhappy child

who tossed coins of hope
for a better existence
and created dreams
of happier times to come

The life she had with him
glorious days of love
the quiet times of care
the wholesome arms
that soothed her
the life, the love, now lost
and splattered before
her weary eyes

Oh, but the well
the waters of hope
the ripples of dreams
that brought her him
could bring him back
or so it seemed

So she hurled her life
and tossed the coin
sobbed and waited
as a storm brewed
and rain poured
washing her wishes
with flooded drops
of realization and regret

She wanted to jump
into this echoing pit
to end the useless pain
Too weak to move
she lay soaked
at the mouth of the well
wishing to be swallowed
For there was no life
without him

The Forest

Around and around

Head tilted towards the sky
hazy breaks of sun beams
wash a cherub face in golden light
that filters through tall trees
forming circular, upward arrows
that dart into the clear blue
with leaves waving in the breeze
too far up to reach
but never too far for dreams to climb
sway like silent wind chimes

around and around

soft hair blowing, jacket flying
a windmill of loose arms
creates a breeze of brown dust
earth disturbed by dancing feet
drunk with nature
this spirit of light
wanders and plays
singing carefree songs
that nestle in the heart
and etch memories in the mind

around and around

what a beautiful day
to discover the forest
and steal a piece of nature
to be forever captured in dreams
a young mind awakens
as the world spins

around and around

By the Stream

Rolling flow

over rocks

smooth

from the run

of white waters

that gurgle

and splash

forging

slippery paths

through sunlit earth

and grassy banks

brown boulders

bathed

in an entrancing

wash of sound

that steeps

in the mind

and fills the body

made up of

such liquid

the core

of waters pure

the clear divide

where nature

and I meet

by the stream

Confused

Believe me
if you please
I'm on my knees
not to acknowledge
my plight
'Cause if you ask me
I will tell you
everything is alright
but oh, so wrong
I am barely holding on
to an ounce of sanity
vanity has me
walking a fine line
on a thin slope
hanging myself
by my own colored rope
I can't cope
emotions are draining me
don't know where to turn
life has me twisted
this heartache burns
don't know what to do
or what I want
or how to make it happen
or how to move forward
randomly turning pages
in the book of my life
sliding on slick covers
masking chapters of strife
skipping paragraphs
not reading the warning signs
You know,
those bright neon lights
written between the lines
hiding the truth from myself
blinded by its glare
I cover it up and
pretend it's not there
no, everything is
copasetic and cool
But I know
I am riding the curb
while playing the fool
so confused...

Metro Scene

Clocking his watch
as he made slow paces
between lamp post
and metro stop
a bouquet of red sunflowers
in hand
dangling to their death
almost touching the ground
as he took out his phone
and frantically dialed
"Where is she?"

Ring tone heard
phone answered
in a calm voice
as she strolled
down the street
on 4 inch heels
and smoothly approached
her annoyed suitor
walked just beyond him
turned and cooed
"Are those for me?"
with a wink and a smile
that soothed his wrinkled
and vexed disposition
flat, yet he gasped
"You are late!"

She just chuckled and smiled
took a whiff of her flowers
rubbed his hand
and proclaimed
"I am well worth the wait"

Terms of Endearment

Terms of negativity
used to degrade
proud warriors and
stellar mothers
into submissive
black hands
that picked cotton and
fed plantations, grand
building houses with
bricks of bigotry
and foundations
of ignorance
to cause or skill
splitting the mentality
of the slave who
digested seeds
of self-hatred
as masters played
shade against shade
the darker the hue
the more arduous
work you do
took pride and
swept it under the rug
as they jumped the broom
with lash whipped skin
that birthed babes
into acceptance
that wore the words

as a scarlet letter
covering soft,
tender hearts
emancipated,
but not free
toting the
master's baggage
as share croppers
and farm hands
a yes sir, yes I can
spit foul terms
out of anger as
seeds bloomed into
giant stalks
of bigotry and
discrimination
that ripped through
a race, divided
a people
and shook a nation
but not enough
to diffuse
names called and
terms owned
that are still heard
in urban ghettos
as demeaning
derogatory
terms of endearment

Lollipop

She tore at the wrapper

'til she held the delight in hand

grabbed the stick and took it in

Letting it dance on her tongue

rolls of flavor licks of love

as she swallowed and sucked

then removed it with a pop of air

her senses erect to the taste

of cherries sweet as Kool Aid

or the love that was made

that still lingered in her hair

the thoughts would not stop

as she teased the lollipop and

all a fellow could do was stare

The Glance: Part I

When eyes met
glances held
just long enough
for two hearts to read
each other's pain
souls embraced
as the second lapsed
the bus pulled past
and out of the gate
It had to be fate
that through
plexi-glass panes
eyes met and hands
seemed to touch
palm to palm
with fingers spread
as a wave of emotions
stirred the urge
no time to think
and in haste
with a surge
mouthed the words
"Stop the bus"
and feet raced
to the gate

They stood
face to face
Speechless
Allowing actions
to be the words
as souls merged
in a calming embrace
more than a hug
more like magic
it was love
As he ran harden
hands over her face
and traced lips
then brow
while wondering
how did this happen
and was this real
The moment revealed
the feelings that filled
two longing hearts
two searching minds
that seem to find
the impossible
at the right time
at the right place…

The Glance: Part II

This love thing brand new
He was desperately seeking
the right things to do
completely drawn in
to new lover and friend
that tugged at his heart
and caught him in a tail-spin
a whirlwind of emotions
such love and such glee
he was her shelter, her light
all she evoked him to be
the man he knew
was buried inside
the man that saw when
he looked in her eyes
and his heart sung
sweet songs of bliss
as soft lips he touched
and pale cheeks he kissed
He knew this was destined
to be a lifelong desire
so he gathered some wire
from within his tote
took her left hand and
strongly proposed
that they continue this life
and weather the tide
with her as his wife
heart to heart
side by side

She was blind
with tears of joy
that poured from
soft, searching

brown eyes
filled with fever
and surprise
that this man
could recognize
her wants
and fill her needs
She was pleased
as she rest her head
on his chest and
he wrapped loving arms
around her until she felt safe
and way too good
for this to be real
but she melted still
and basked in the exchange
thinking, "he doesn't even
know my last name"
It wasn't given or stated
they were so
swept away with
conversation
lasting for hours
that seemed days
They connected in ways
only written in plays
This new love a haze
a sonnet, something
she knew she wanted
inhibitions aside
she was ready to ride
on a whim and a prayer
on this blessed day
so in his arms she lay
one word left to say...
Yes!

Beauty

Perception

intuitive recognition

appreciation

the perfect imperfection

endearing

sensory manifestation

deep satisfaction

divine revelation

a concept, a collective

grace of nature

stateliness

landscapes or environments

spirituality

truthfulness

harmony and artistry

gratifying

attractive

wonderful

comeliness

extraordinary

meaningful

pleasing in appearance

What is beauty, I must ask,
and in what state does it exist?

In the Shower

In the shower
I sing myself awake
cleansing my mind in tune
bathing my flesh
As water runs down breast and back

In the shower

Scented soaps are therapists
invigorating aromas and
calming body balms
Tell me everything will be alright

In the shower

I riverdance in a pool of purpose
Jump in the mist of my life
stomp off trials
Beat my cares down the drain

In the shower

I lather self love
rinse tears of sorrow
wash away past pain
allowing the water to quench
my thirst for renewal

In the shower

Dementia

This stranger I know has been on my mind
Its been a long time since we last spoke.
Several years have gone by and I can't gather the courage
to be a foreigner in the house where I was raised.
I don't want to put the key in the door and not hear a chuckle
"It must be about to snow!"

The house is unkept now. It used to be pristine
Down on hands and knees I would dig debris out of corners
and wipe baseboards, beat dirt out of rugs and
clean the bathroom 'til you could eat off the floors.
No filth missed cause Grandma could spot dirt clear across the room.
"Better get that mop and start again," she'd chime in.
She nursed me through illnesses with home remedies
of cod liver oil, epson salts and iodine
Sung at the stove when preparing dinner
that was promptly served at 4:00 everyday but, Saturday's
"Every man for himself and God for us all"

Keen and wise, my young mind she molded
taught me to "Keep my dress down and legs closed".
She slapped sense into me with a dish rag,
disciplined my disobedience with a thick switch, and
chased me down the street with a fly swatter
if I did not make it in before the street lights came on.
But she always managed to show me love

Dementia (continued)

She encouraged me to push through college
And gave me words of wisdom to carry when I wed
She was the only one who believed in my art
Looked my father in the eye and declared
"She is going to be an artist."
She cried tears of pride and joy when I gave her a
painted portrait of my deceased grandfather
and she hung it on the wall next to their bed
"I talk to it every night," she said.

I spent so much of my life looking up to her
I don't want to see her down
I cannot bare to witness her healthy body
living in a world of jumbled and lost memories.
The woman who once lived so bold and free
calls her son, "The man that brings her food"
and her daughter, "The nice lady that visits".
I know that she will never know my son's name
and she has long forgotten that I exist
I can't stomach the thought of her looking at me
and asking "Who are you?"
So I stay away and hide in my memories.

In the Ruff

He dwells in the elements
that compound his life
A product of the environment
to which he was born
accepted, not chosen
He lives on hard grounds
He hides a razor sharp mind
behind malice and scorn
He has a rugged exterior
that is hard to break
He is a diamond
living in the worldly ruff
Not distinguishable from the
glass shards and fakes
He is perceived as
unpolished and tough
Though it is a common mistake
If only he'd look past his coating
To the brilliance that shines within
He'd live up to his fullest potential
and shine like the diamond he is

Another Year

I celebrate my life given

as I live to see another year

rich with blessings

filled with lessons

taught and learned

God has renewed and restored

brought me full circle

back to the woman I know

Has given me breath of purpose

and shown me the beauty

that living can bring

Although I have had

my share of sorrows

I am glad to say

I have seen more joy

I take this day of birth

not as an extension

of dreaded years

But as a beacon

a reminder of the many

who are not here

and to appreciate the time

and privilege granted to live

House Cleaning

I am cleaning out the closet

Pulling out those skeletons

Giving them a once over

And then tossing them in the trash

I am dusting the cobwebs of artistic thoughts

left in the corners of my mind

Placing them in the forefront of

Things to be accomplished

I am mopping the floors of my heart

Eliminating tracked in dirt and grime

Scrubbing with elbow grease

To make room for love

I am washing the windows of my soul

Windexing my foresight

Wiping up the tears impairing my perception

To be alert in my infinite surroundings

Yes, I am cleaning house

And continuing in life, renewed

Sometimes...

Sometimes I feel the urge
>   To call you up and curse you out
>   Wrap my words around your throat
>   And choke you until my head feels free

But that would just make a fool of me.

Sometimes I feel the urge
>   To kick you off of your porcelain pedestal
>   Stomp you out of your purple haze
>   And have you face the error of your ways

But I'm not judge or jury except on my own faulted path.

Sometimes I feel the urge
>   To punch you where I know it hurts
>   Left jab to selfish pride
>   Right hook into your poker face of lies
>   And knock you into being an honest man

But I am no superwoman and it is time that you realize.

The Undercurrent

Deep, below the surface
under the eddy of words
mixed in the course of actions
lies the powerful suggestions
and riveting connotations
that make up the flux of poems
heard, in a screaming whisper

Once held by a rickety sluice
the waters broke free of line
in an outpour of love, rage and soul
that now flows as the torrid blue
of my mind's eye and my heart's ear

As the gush of thoughts
the emanation of emotions
the tides of my existence
The undercurrent of my life

Common Situation: A Short Story

Her stomach bubbled as she sat in the smooth, black chair. She pushed strands of hair out of view as she tapped the silvery mouse. Mind racing, heart pounding; she checked the room several times before placing her hands on the keys and typing in the url.

She just had to know what she really did not want to. Bright page popped up with several recorded entries of paperless mail that still left a trail. Each adorned with a pretty face smiling through deception. Those perfect white teeth that snared her heart and gnawed through her unrequited perception of love. Her love.

His words screamed off the screen.

Her heart fell at her feet.

She turned and heaved

She could not breath.

How could he live with such deceit?

Typed confessions of love and sex. Passion that had long left her longing arms and empty heart. She recalled nights apart when he was so close but never near. Late nights working, the fights, the tears. All of her fears brought to light. And oh, she must endure the night for he was not to return home until three in the early morn.

Where did I go wrong?

What did I do?

What does she have that I can't provide for you?

How can this be?

I gave years of my life.

So you could turn to that?

LISTEN, I am your wife!

Common Situation: A Short Story (continued)

The words soared like knives down the hall, piercing his afterglow high. Moments ago, he had died in a pillow of thighs and held pleasure in his palms. Cupping the vociferous calm of her body so warm, open and free. Free of commitment, free of bills, free of the pull of rationality. There was no gravity of life weighing him down. He sailed the skies and leaped buildings in a single bound. He was the warrior, the conqueror, the slayer, the knight. All that he could not be in the eyes of his wife.

He kneeled to the papers thrown at his feet, aimed for his head. Picked up the pretty printed picture and said, "What I have with her now is something long lost between us two. She makes me feel alive, revitalized, brand new. There is no sting or strings tying me to promises I have yet to keep. She tells me everything is alright and kisses me deep. She holds me in my sleep!"

"GIVE IT TIME", she chimed in, "and you will find that in reality your life, so weightless and free, is not all it's cracked up to be. She will want your decision, your love and definition of the relationship you are in. She'll want more than sex and more sex, she'll want a commitment. And we both know the route you choose when faced with the fire, the coward you are and lives you ruin to fill your own selfish desires. Yes, she will find herself in my boat, wounded and scarred. Barely afloat, but with enough sass and class to do as I am and put you out on your ass. Get your things, take this ring and get out of this house!"

"Mommy, is everything okay?" cried a small voice from the stairs. Sad little eyes gleamed from behind rustled hair.

"Daddy, you are home! I missed you! Are you about to leave? But you just got here. Come and read to me. Please!"

"Mommy, don't cry, I will kiss your tears away. Just don't make Daddy leave. I want you both to stay"...

Empty Space

Sometimes I go to the quiet place

The place within my soul

and feel the void

the empty spot where

silence lingers and love awaits

The numb spot that throbs

and longs to be fulfilled

The place where you should be

And though I don't know

who you are

My heart knows that you exist

and will one day fill your place

with the light of your love

The numb will fade

my heart will soar

and my soul will have its peace

Take the Lead

Take my hand and direct me

to life's dance floor

If you guide me with sure feet

how can we stray?

Lead me with steps, ordered

I am willing to follow

and join you in love's twirl

Sweep me away

as I pirouette off my feet

and find comfort

in your trusted embrace

Let us dance

through the many songs of life

arm in arm, hand in hand

In the Eye of the Beholder

You are beautiful...

Echoed in the wind and
rang in the ears of two
unsuspecting recipients
> He may have seemed slow to some, not quite well, perhaps
> While telling the world of his path and plans for the day
> But in that moment that he beheld the two chatting faces
> he felt compelled, out of the trance of plans
> ringing in disabled ears, to utter the words
> mirrored by the beckoning smiles of passersby...

You are beautiful...

She heard from the foot
of the railed bed in which she lay
Her face throbbed and her heart ached
more for each cut, sliced across
what was once her face
Nose displaced, eyes torn, cheeks swollen
tissues bloated and bruised
her body abused by no man's love
and her man's hate, it wasn't fate
that ripped hair from scalp and
punched imprints in skin
replacing vibrancy with battered bones of mind
> And yet she finds her true love by her side
> soothing her scarred heart as he holds her fractured hand
> and lets the words wrap about her tethered frame...

You are beautiful...

The world screams: BEAUTY is far more than
in the eye of the beholder.

In the Still

By the light of the umber moon
beneath the howl of the wanton wind
in the still of a thought-filled midnight
my spirit is nourished and I feed
by the damp, firm earth and
dew kissed leaves and
happy songs of bluejays that fly with me
as my soul soars on heartstrings
like feathers gently blown
from God's soft, extended hands
and I hear him calling me
under the whisper of the stars
on the gleaming waves of a silent sea
in the watchful eyes of nature's owl
my spirit set my mind's woes free
in the quiet still of a thought-filled midnight

Cry

Let the waters flood

Let each tear fall

Let sorrow pass

and break the troubled wall

Let your heart find peace

Let your spirit breath

Let your mind be released

and set your worries at ease

Cry like the world is ending

Cry when new life's beginning

Cry when you need to grieve

Just cry and find your soul's relief

I Want to Be...

I want to be...

The source of your late night, restful slumber

The comforting thought nestled in your mind

The cunning vixen in your sexiest dreams

I want to be...

Your playmate in mischief

The cool of your swagger

That fire that brings you the heat, but never burns

I want to be...

All in your hair

Embedded in your bones

So much more than I am to you, right now

I want to be...

Yours.

More Than Intuition

I know you...

You tend to cover complacency
with blankets thrown over your cold heart
The warmth escaped you in lost love's wind
that blew in seeds of her deception
that spawned and planted gigantic weeds
nourished in a twisted forest in your heart
clogging arteries and blocking love

You seek hide in this jungle
to avoid anxiety over possible pain
No love, no faith, no relationships
Not willing to take a chance or a flying leap
The vines of heart a noose around your neck
and have you swinging in your air of loneliness
suffocating in your state of mind

I want to cut the rope and pull you in
to where I know you haven't the will to go
I want to be the lifeline pumping victory
in your veins and clearing your arteries
of the fatty mess she made
But you won't allow me to get close
enough to let my oxygenated love flow
You only want me from a distance
on call with love juice and confidence pills
when the weeds are too high to climb
and the lonely vines cause heartache for affection
I stand on top and cut them down
until you are frightened and shoo me away
only to call me to the door without letting me in
over and over again.

Yes, I know you, oh too well.

Sacrifice

She runs on the wind

Feet soaring above brown earth

A dust storm blowing behind her rapid pace

She makes dreams goals and goals history

with the wind in her hair and the stars in her eyes

There is nothing impossible, no race she can't run

for the sacrifice was made long before she knew breath

and learned she could run with the birds and walk in the sky

For Troy: Reciprocity

We will never be together
in black and white photos
hands extended with matching rings
I won't wear the smiles of your love on my face or
sport blushing cheeks from your embrace

We won't wake day by day
to the light in each others eyes
Nor will I often listen
to the calm melody of your heart
beating as I lay on your chest

I won't hold your tongue or
feel your lips the way I have longed
and three words will not cuddle in my ears
Yet, I am not afraid to love you
and not fearful to care

But I won't wait for magic
to break its holding spell
on your tangled life
For even the strongest of hearts
knows love is idol if it is not returned

Risk to Love

Go out on love's limb

yell at the moon and sing to the leaves

Hop, skip, jump on love's tightrope

make steady your pace as the truth sets you free

Bungie jump, free fall, paraglide into passion

there's no other plunge like falling in love

Surf, sail, powerski on love's waters

with all the abandon that dreams are made of

Take hold and grasp the spirit of adventure

Dare to be committed, open, and true

Know you take risks for any love or achievement

Don't shy away from the blessings that love has for you

Fall in Love

Give Love

Receive Love

Be Loved ... Just Love

Goodbye Blues

No more gloomy blues

I planted them deep

within the grounds

on which I stand

I watered them with

tears of relief

drowned them in sunshine

added mulch of life experience

and knowledge of my mistakes

Fertilized them with self love

and pulled up weeds of self doubt

used my green thumb of purpose

to color my world with substance

and grew flowers in my garden

in a new, beautiful hue

Complex Simplicity

You ...

    Avoid without abstaining

    Desire without wanting

    Eradicate without breaking

    Hold without loving

    Justify without apologizing

    Lend without giving

    Reserve without retaining

    State without explaining

    Take without grasping

    View without seeing

Exist without being.

Inside Me

Inside out

You take me

Feel me

breath me

I feel the burn

that moves beyond lust

internal combustion

with each thrust

my heart beats faster

breaths are heavier

the want, the need

the passion, the greed

making love

to my brain

euphoric, erotic

sensations

hot blood in my veins

you push me

twist me

please me

feed me

fill the need in me

welcome, inside me

A Good Read

He is an open book
stunning jacket, vivid pages
I read him cover to cover
decipher the hidden phrases
between the sheets
resting on the lines
his story unwinds
but do I comprehend
follow his flow and
soak the words in?
take time to find meaning
as the story unfolds
being ever mindful
of the emphasis in bold
I need to read and
heed the disclaimers
rise and fall at his story's peak
thumb through the index
let the prose speak
the volume of his heart
and the troubles of his mind
see past the gold letters
written on his spine
I'm trying not to skip ahead
and miss poignant paragraphs
and revealing chapters
the hurt, the joys
the heartfelt laughter
Yes, he is a good book
and I am intrigued
so I dive in and continue to read

Horsepower

It doesn't matter

if you have a hypersonic car

with the greatest horsepower

on the speedway of life

if you are a feeble

and incompetent driver.

For all the horses in the world

won't mean a thing!

The Performance

It was hot beneath
the blazing lights
she began to perspire
as she slowly
stepped to the mic
and inhaled the crowd
of hundreds
of cheers and smiles
chatter silenced
the time was now
she opened her mouth
and exhaled
her lifelong melody
she pushed
out of her mind
and sung with her body
strain on her face
her words erased
all her pain
as she began to sing
the whole world
went away

Diaphram belted
harmonious notes
voicing rhyme
filled with emotion
holding the crowd
on each line
her throat the funnel
for spewing feelings

on treble clef wings
off of the stage
evoking the listeners
to sway to love
and engage

This was the day
her mama said she'd see
this was the day
she lived out her dreams
under the lights
as bright as
the midnight moon
alone with the mic
the performance
would be over soon

She sang
using the blessings
God gave her

She sang
as if no one else
could hear her

She sang
with all her
strength and might

She sang
for singing
was her life

Signals

We all are turn signals
of the cars of life
blinking to our own rhythms
while navigating our plights

Some are lefties
Hitting life's corners with ease
Making rounds to the straight
and narrow while
basking in the breeze

Some are righties
Gotta get a good grip to turn
Steering wheel spinning
Jumping the curb, yet managing,
somehow, to live and learn

Some are hazards
Pulled to the shoulder, boiled over
Don't know which way to go
Begging to be seen while
pondering life and all it means

Some are busted
Holding for hope, forlorn and tired
Hanging on by a measly wire
Barely functioning, sporadic glow
Wind battered, broken and exposed

Yes, we all are turn signals
Hoping to synchronize
in a never ending chorus
of life, love and blinking lights

Next Stop, Farragut North!

He shifted uneasily
adjusted his tie and
cleared his throat.
The scent of her perfume
tickled his nose as she
hovered above him.
He clenched the seat rail
as her hand brushed his
sending a chill up his spine.
She looked down and smiled.

"What a lovely smile..."
Doors opening!

People rushing, hustling about
with briefcases and baggage.
Yet, he was focused
on her blouse
with visions of copping a feel
in the tunnel or her legs
against his waist on the door.

"Whew...shake it off," he thought.

Next stop Tenleytown!
His seat neighbor exited.

"May I sit here?" she asked,
as she slid past
and sat down next to him.
Her long curls gently swept
across his cheek and
her soft leg touched him
ever so lightly.

"Oh my God!" he thought,
"Why are you torturing me?"

Soft music playing
in the background
from a nearby iPOD.
People getting on
and getting off.
All he could think of
was the latter.

He pulled out his cell
attempting to divert
his attention but
the air was on blast and
her nipples were hard.
He tried to focus
out of the window
only to find a grand view
of a cement wall and
the better view
of her reflection.

He moved his briefcase to his lap.
"Farragut North,
will you ever come?" he thought.

The rail lights flashed
and he felt a tongue
wash over his lips.
"I will see you tonight
and I don't have
any panties on..."
is what she left him with.

Convicted

NavWorks Press (MySpace) one list poetry challenge:

Write and post one or more poems of any length, size, or style using every word in the following list in each poem written:

astound	electric	subversive
reduce	gouge	euphoric
instigate	eradicate	climb
	trial	

I should be on trial

for the euphoric feelings

and the electric currents that

climb across lands of my skin

You instigate and fuel my desires

leave me astounded by your abilities

to drive me far beyond the point of passion

that eradicates my sense of stability leaving me

hanging on each word your luscious mouth utters

If this be sin, gouge out my heart and reduce me

to the sinner's paradise of your wide subversive arms

For I am enticed by the mere, fleeting thought of your love

Walk of Life

One cloudy day
I journeyed for the horizon

on a walk of wooden trail
cast far into the sea

that beckoned me:
forward, move forward

quiet waves whispered
secrets I dispelled to the wind

the crisp air cleansed
my broken spirit,
restored my inner peace

the sea sprays washed
my cares between the planks
and soothed my tired feet

earth and sky
board and sea
for miles and miles

still I journeyed on
each step growing in ease
as the horizon drew nearer

Forward, move forward
Freedom awaits you…

Ode to Jimi

The man was nice
with fingers that glided
like ice on skin
up and down
hitting chords
shook the floor
had them begging for more
screaming
baby rock my boat
as guitar strings
hit sweet notes
fingering love
strumming joy
letting freedom ring
as he sweat
from the lights
above the stage
songbird uncaged

his fingers enraged
the performance, wet
vibing to the beat
playing the sweetest set
of funky music
on her silhouette
as good as it gets
electric pulse
streamed to the rhythm
feeling the amps
he had that good
soul filled music
put you in a trance
rocked your world
as you were unfurled
by that sweet guitar
and his skillful hands
Yes, he was the man

Soaring

You aren't up
just tryin to bring me down
reaching, grabbing
but I am up too high
your arms too short
to reach the sky
I am climbing heights
and no man is
gonna bring me down
I have solid resound
in convictions I found
a long time ago
you should know
this is no ordinary trip I'm on
I've soared beyond
seen the horizon
living life in the skies
reflecting on the
stormy days
there are no tears
in my eyes
I look forward in truth
travel on the path
that I set
navigate the heights
weather the storms
bask in the sunlight
and walk in the wind
I will continue
this soaring journey
until my humble life ends
so don't drag me down
into your mess
just let me fly
onward with lifted wings
until the day I die

Her Groove

She walked in
grin on her face
smooth was her glide
she sighed, ambrosia
all over the place
she stood with grace
had enough spunk to
knock a player down
her eyes light brown
her appeal was sex
it oozed down her spine
past her hips
had men hanging
on her every line
every time she
parted her lips or
batted her eyes
she could make a
grown man cry
her whole body
was curves
um, yes she was fine
tailor made
platinum package
intervention divine
She was holding
no baggage
toting no carts
had been known
amongst the grown
to steal a few hearts
and pull a string or two
they'd step back and watch
her "do the thing she do"
as she laughed aloud
and charmed the crowd
with her socialite skills
the type of hype that
could go out with the girls
or stay home and chill
but enjoyed a good flirt
considered it a thrill
she could get what she
wanted if said
in a soothing tone
but with all those
qualities owned
why was she alone?

Attraction

This intensity, magnetism
draws me in   enthralled

You look my way and
I can't hold your stare

Or you will read the desires
of my soul and feel the passionate

vibes riding on chemical waves   inhaled
that race through my bloodstream

I want to
I want you

Not now, not for just a mere moment
I want to ride your mind

have you taste me in your dreams
long before your tongue has its pleasure

Kiss you without touching lips
hold you without use of limbs

reach well beyond attraction
into the core of need

I want you
I truly want you

to want me

In the Hole

Jumped in that hole
10,000 feet too deep
to climb free
too steep to hurdle
no rope to pull
no hook to catch
this life's a mess
you clean it up to only
get sucked back in
can't get the monkey
off your shoulders
and pull yourself out of that hole
get your life back on track
and learn to solve financial woes
with the pennies you have left
and the money you could not save
not knowing how to meet your goals
and own a home one day
with cracked credit and
extra high percentage rates
it is work to get ahead
dreams start to fade
financial stress

an upward climb
on an slippery slope
feet skidding, backsliding
slowly giving up hope
creditors haggling
calling you constantly
bidding for your last dime
that you spent a week
and 100 dollars ago
to pay that parking fine
these are hard times
arduous work for 15 cent
credit cards, child care
gasoline, rent
car payments, utilities
groceries, insurance
by the time the check is cut
all the money's spent
no way to get ahead
no resources to lend
no ladder to ascend
when will this headache
ever end?

The End's Beginning

Tears fall, words hail
like bullets
through the moiling
atmosphere
of love's crashing sky
Adrenaline high
screams slap cheeks
and accusations hurl
punches and blows
that leave hearts sore
and minds aching
Hands shaking
pointed fingers
that poke holes
through veracity
jeering comments
tight clenched teeth
the gnashing and biting
"why don't you listen to me?"
Can't see through opaque eyes
open only to passion's fury
the huddled hurt and
tantrum of trifles
erupt anger
in an outrage of words

None heard
falling on hard heads
and stubborn dispositions
Not to mention
holding nothing
giving much less
than their propensity
to yell too much
Enough is enough
joy remiss
bliss long gone
sewing seeds of
worry and hate
this house is no home
I must move on
box up the fury
push past the fear
grab hold of the keys
get the hell out of here
the end is near
and I'd rather be alone
than to suffer
in your presence
when I can do bad
on my own

Getting to Know You

I could let desire be my navigator
row your boat without an oar
leave friendship in the wind
while setting sail on lust-filled seas

I could let nature take its course
as we come together at a rapid pace
Ride the sex wave and allow the passion
to rush in like the rolling tide

I could spread like eagle wings
from your slightest touch
Purr softly as fingers
trace lines over delicate skin

I could let bodies merge
while getting to know you
well before I know of you
get high off the excitement
and the risks we take

But we both know that is not all
that I really want...

So...
I should take my time to understand you
learn of where your ship is sailing
hear of journeys of your past and
oceans you have yet to claim

find my place amongst your crew
while we learn to sail the seas together
striving for peace at shore
and as equal peace of mind

no rush
no push
no lack-luster lines
just an honest attempt
to get to know you

The Web We Weave

Shiny threads

intriquitly held in place

just so

spread out

in a form for all to see

delicate beads of past

kiss over lines

like dew drops on leaves

glimmering

as the loom spins gently

and tiny spools release

the silky strings of thought

into glistening webs

of memory

Spellbound

Spellbound, it's quiet now

lingering thoughts of you and me

fill my mind like the musk of sex in the air

Bare legs and thighs

entertwined on the cuff of the bed

The calm of this moment

such a turn from the last

where bodies lashed out for affection

mutual attraction, burning desire

softly seduced as we both aimed to please

Pleasure was abundant, indeed

as you cast heartfelt phrases in my ear

as I listened to you die in my lap

with a wave of your wand

And here we are

full-service satisfied

spellbound, in the quiet

of a night full of passion

Lesson Learned

I was naive
thought the world was love
and you were my world
Your spherical axis of actions
spun me deep in emotion's magma
your gravitational pull, pulled me in
sucked me into your atmosphere
and all I allowed you to mean
while I floated in the space between us

I thought this was how love is
no sun, no stars just dark and dust
shattered fragments of dreams lost
and love abandoned
I wished for a moonbeam, shooting star
sign of affection, the glisten of hope
or sparkle of truth
to no avail
love cannot live in a heart of stone

It took me light-years and lonely days
to realize I was on this ship alone
there was no satellite of communication
no comet to ride to spark the fire in you, so
I journeyed beyond the moon of your presence
and left your memories in Saturn's rings
Let time and space heal me
and show me a new path home

Grounded and wiser
I seek not love in another, but give love
with reciprocity, knowing the world is love
when you truly have love for yourself

Long Gone

I stand ajar

heart open

my body at bay

come float with me

I want to see

that look in your eyes

the one that takes me there

the one that haunts me

in my loftiest dreams

come and feel this

there are no handles

to carry this want

no box to hold it

no lid to capture

raw desire

the door is open

close it behind you

shut off the phone

and lose yourself in me

for I was long gone

way before you came

Playing with Fire

The fire rages with
a flux of love oxygen
not one to play with
I burn through bullshit
consume fear
I am a firestarter
piromaniac
with open flame
orange flickering
burning fire
blazing hot
searing mentality
scorching tongue
that blue light lit
on the end of your wick
dancing sparks
soaring in wind
devouring inhibition
fueled by desire
ignited by the fingers
of your right hand
that skims skin
and causes night sweats
in your sleep
from the memory of
my sweltering heat

the fire rages within
come put me out

Love's Decay

sharp tongue

bit straight to the bone

tore at the flesh

ground the gristle —

caused the kind of aching

novacaine can't numb —

left a foul taste

in a closed mouth

and the rotting teeth

of love's decay

Cocky

If I could only be

a peacock's feather

bold, colored, oval pattern

turquoise, royal and umber silken strands

standing upward, on point, to the sky

while I wisp whimsically through airs

held only by a stem of pride

viewed as a fan of glory

a crown of decadence

spread out for the world to see

captured in brilliance in your mind

as the daunting, delicate beauty   I am

Not Your Melody

I don't want to be your melody

I want to be sung in harmony
the intricate and moving composition
the cool notes that slide from your throat
like the sexy wail of a saxophone

I want to be the heat of the rhythm
the pulse of your every beat
played vibrato sung staccato
in accord with the music we create

I want to be that special verse
the one that evokes tears of joy
and moments of remembrance
that play on your mind in a loop

I want the world to feel me
as you sing my chords
and let your fingers speak
through the silky keys

I want our song to be
the breath you breathe
and the air I take in
as our song sails in the wind

I want it to fill our space with love
billowing in the quiet of candlelit nights
and the bright light of sunny days
to be sung forever in many different ways

No, I don't want to be your melody
that line was "so" yesterday

Hustler

thirty years, thirty years
I've been at this playa
for some odd thirty years
You don't know my struggles
or the way that I feel
lest you're living the life I live...

I hit the streets when I was fifteen
Cause my mama couldn't keep
her legs down or nose clean
Squeaky springs and moans
as I huddled in a corner all alone
A far cry from home
our apartment was poison
cocaine on the table
pipes by the sink
needles in the toilet
no food, no lights
nothing to drink
Mama wasn't around to
kiss me goodnight or tuck me in
her time was spent
snorting, cussing and sucking
miscellaneous men for a dime
left me to fend for myself
I turned to a life of crime
Thought it was the only way
for a young black ghetto boy
to gain loot and be paid

slinging rocks and bagging weed
I took to the streets
threw on this hard ass hustle
determined to see more
than the ghettos front door
I wanted that plush house
and dope ride so I
took to slinging the same rock
that stole my moms from this life
you'd have thought I learned
from her struggles and strife
But I closed my heart
and shut my eyes
I thought the world was mine
for the taking until the day when
I sold that good shit to the man
spent 3 years in the can
my first felony
went right back to the block
to start making that money
and fooling with the honeys
I wasn't around to attend
my mother's funeral
or witness the birth of my daughter
I was still caught in the
hard lesson life was teaching
But I was never one
to do what I ought to
constantly reaching to obtain

Hustler (continued)

riches, and bitches
and have everyone know my name
I wrote the game
had street fame
that bred hatred
in those wanting what I got
so, I was flossing in my caddy
when I heard gun shots
bullet by my heart
and one in my lung
you'd have thought I was done
knowing how close I'd come
to dying, yet I was still trying
to perfect this hustle
Not realizing there was no
gain in this struggle
just bloodshed and tears
and before I knew it
I'd been at it for
thirty years, thirty years
damn, I've been at this playa
for some odd thirty years
You don't know my struggles
or the way that I feel
lest you're living the life I live
this shit is real
I wrote this game a long time ago
I'm a hustler baby, survivor
so much more than the man
you think you know

Now and Then

you blow in

the breeze

of my thoughts

come and go

like the ebb of the tide

I hear your voice

in the echoing halls of mind —

saccharine words cast

down the bony stairs of my spine

to hallow rooms at heart

though, you are no kind wind

for one forlorn of commitment —

osculating stale air about

touched with the scent

you leave behind

Reflection: Distant

350 miles apart...

the spoon clinks against the cup

stirring my emotions

I grab and hug a soft pillow, tightly

I shift uneasily

trying to focus

on the murmur of voices, blurred faces

from the television screen

"there's that damn clinking again!"

slurped sips of hot liquid

blood boiling in my veins

in vain

insane

that he is sitting

right next to me

on this couch

and we are

350 miles apart

Request: Understanding

This love has me
falling like Autumn leaves
afraid of strong winds
I follow the flow but
I'm too scared to let you in
so I rake emotions
into piles of denial
compost strewn
over fragile, tender places
I'm not open for
this level of love
with all the challenges
we are faced with
chasing the dream
that leaves me hanging
floating in somber skies
swinging on your words
open ended
freshly exposing
raw nerves to
the crisp Fall air
creating an ache
that will not quell

yet I manage to bear
the plagues of
my insecurities
silence my timorous cry
and allow your love
to whisper sweet nothings
and see through
transparent eyes
open wide

I pray you...
teach my heart like the
seasons illustrate change
to embrace the inevitable
and follow the bright red hue
imbued in the veins of love
so when the leaves crumple
to dust and the winter
has had its way
Our love will flower
in the spring of life
and stand under the warmth
of understanding

Not Made for Walking

I stepped into
these heels
with intentions

No, these shoes
aren't of the
walking kind

I want you
to drink
in my legs
follow the rise
of my calves
and the rounds
of my back
see my hips
sway as I
glide your way

No, these shoes
aren't of the
walking kind

tall, black stilettos
working wonders
for my thighs
breast bouncing
to my beat
with every smooth
step I take
sexy, curvaceous
dangerous
with full intent

No, baby
these shoes
aren't of the
walking kind

Southbound

We travel the
county roads
that are lined with
wooden shacks
Escalades in the
front yard, dirt
and clothes lines
in the back
miles and miles
of earth and trees
quiet roads
and sun hot breeze
old folks sitting
on the porche

we make way
through town
where dogwoods sing
and bright azaleas dance
look in awe at
plantation houses
that were built
with strong
black hands
a smile of pride
at that thought
followed by
a sigh of despair
that there aren't many
of the builders kind
living in the area

In the bottom
there is a church
and a package store on
every cornered street
folks hanging around
sitting on porches
sweating from the heat
shorty and y'all and
I'm fixin'-to-go
language that you hear
with a hey and a
I ain't stud'ing you
now go and
fetch me a beer

riding in the car
listening to
booty shake and
good ole' down
home blues
watching the rise and fall
of rolling hills and
sweating in the
heat of June
there is a level of pride
I can't deny
when I think
of my southern home
that is so much
a part of me and
the memories that I own

Absence of Mind

I wish out of sight
was always out of mind
cause thoughts of you
have been plaguing me all day
like the way your lip
curls when you smile
or how you gently bite it
when thinking dirty thoughts
and oh, the looks you throw me
and the way you
touch my hair and
kiss my thighs
You know I love
the look in your eyes

whew, no, I can't get you off of my mind

I smell you in my dreams
picture your body taunting me
your image plays
in my head all day
I hear your voice and get chills
just imagining
your breath hovering
over my breasts
the way you stand
statuesque at my
bedroom door
the way you pull me closer
and wheel me in
and the bliss of you
inside me, beside me

I wish you were here
I long for you, here
but since you are
no where near
I could really use
an absence of mind

Live...

soft spoken secrets
whispers of love and kind
the type of tales dreams are made of
that breed hope in barren minds

soft, glittering, glowing ideas
dispelled in the air of thought
and the breath of reason
soul soaring, life-changing,
lightening bug flickers
of moments yet captured
beyond the mind's existence
gleaming in the night, heard
and gently break the quiet
so dreams become reality
and actions spring from intent

cast your secrets in the midnight air
and relish in the grandeur of your dreams

spread your wings, soar and live

Thinking of Yesterday

Yesterday
would have awakened me
with a soft, caring kiss on the forehead
and whispered sweet nothings in my ear
while shooting looks of lust and love
across the pillows on the bed

Yesterday
would have held my hand in public
extended his arm when taking a stroll
walked on the outside of the sidewalk
held the door as we entered
and helped me get into the car

Yesterday
would have made love in abandon
expressed emotions with blatant truth
worked towards goals with perseverance
strived for prospects of the future
and still made time to spend with me

Yesterday
would have made our love a top priority
pushed his drama to the side
evoked feelings both warm and real
sought the pleasure of my company
blessed my life with the joy of his

Yesterday
would have never let me walk away...
evolved into Today
no affection, no respect, no joy and no love
the warm fuzzy feeling is gone and
it is so hard to say goodbye to...

Things I Believe

I believe in love

I believe in God

I believe in peace

I believe in good

I believe in respect

I believe in dreams

I believe in change

I believe in gratitude

I believe in resilience

I believe in persistence

I believe in learning

I believe in truth

I believe in blessings

I believe in happiness

I believe in myself

I believe in you

Dare to believe!

Phobic

He pushed gently, without shoving
not allowing his conscious to hold
what his heart was hoping for
waiting for

Afraid of the surge of emotions
that her presence lent

He quietly withdrew into
his spinning thoughts and heavy heart
as uneasy words fell from his weary lips

"I don't want this love"

Afraid to commit
even more scared to abandon the hurt
he climbed into the amor of work
and under a blanket of distance

Letting no one near

Missing out on countless blessings

Groveling in misery

Suffering in lost love's pain

Can't Find the Words

I reach inward

as you, *the pulley*

draw me deep

into your groove

hook, line, and sinker

inside pink flesh, *smooth*

lay over

frozen hard emotions

that are quickly melting

from the heat of your drive

following rhythmic motions

I am out of my mind

trying to dispell words

for this indescribable feeling

natural, sensual, high

Yes! Making me

want to sing

and write

and snuggle

in the loving warmth

of *you*

Where I Need to Be

Take me there
Yes, I mean
Right There

You know
to the place
where comfort
is luxury
and luxury is
abundant
and the healing
oh the healing
is warm, warm
and free
free of i's and you's
and it's about me
free of stereotypes
and fake hype
Free to just be
in the nest of we
where we reside
and longing is to feel
fill each others needs
and needs are
more like wants
sought not in greed

Yes, love is bestowed
in this cove where
thoughts are as beautiful
as life-long dreams
that spring leaves
of promise and
drop seeds of hope
Hope for tomorrow
hope with faith
hope to flourish
as our garden flowers
and ideas bloom
petals of brilliance
petals of kind
that renew our minds and
guide our actions
give direction to intent
where what is said is done
and nothing is said
that is not meant

Oh, you have to
take me there
I want to go there
I know that it exists...
Is it in **you***?*

See What You Did...(explicit?)

Damn boy
your kind of sexy
should be a crime and
you are violating me
6 counts of mental rape
a sentence of love slavery
and you, sex craving me
I'd like to lock you in my legs
and tuck away the key
(seek and you will find)
bodies intertwined
lips on the mind
(your two...all of mine)
soft and wet and
moist and heat
the high glow of your body
the scorching heat of me
(I need a fan...
someone turn on the air)
It is **Hot**
flashes of brain fucks
that mental game we play
and play, and play
you move a little closer
I slide in, then move away

lightly touch your chest
wishing your hands
were on my breasts
massaging my ego
while riding you regal
Kiss you where you
don't want me to
though you so want me to
forget my name
and scream yours
spell it out sing it out
SHOUT it out
hit you with the chorus
(instrumental)
hot sex in my mind's
front lobby
break me off
on the sofa
suck me in
and make it sloppy

ooh you make me wanna
you make me wanna
you make me want to...
ooh ooh oh!

Index of Poems

Life Senses	2
By the Track	3
The Wishing Well	4
The Forest	5
By the Stream	6
Confused	7
Metro Scene	8
Terms of Endearment	9
Lollipop	10
The Glance: I	11
The Glance: II	12
Beauty	13
In the Shower	14
Dementia	15
In the Ruff	17
Another Year	18
House Cleaning	19
Sometimes...	20
The Undercurrent	21
Common Situation: A Short Story	22
Empty Space	24
Take the Lead	25
In the Eye of the Beholder	26
In the Still	27
Cry	28
I Want To Be...	29
More than Intuition	30
Sacrifice	31
For Troy: Reciprocity	32
Risk to Love	33
Goodbye Blues	34
Complex Simplicity	35
Inside Me	36
A Good Read	37
Horsepower	38

Index of Poems

The Performance 39
Signals 40
Next Stop, Farragut North 41
Convicted 42
Walk of Life 43
Ode to Jimi 44
Soaring 45
Her Groove 46
Attraction 47
In the Hole 48
The End's Beginning 49
Getting to Know You 50
The Web We Weave 51
Spellbound 52
Lesson Learned 53
Long Gone 54
Playing with Fire 55
Love's Decay 56
Cocky 57
Not Your Melody 58
Hustler 59
Now and Then 61
Reflection: Distant 62
Request: Understanding 63
Not Made for Walking 64
Southbound 65
Absence of Mind 66
Live 67
Thinking of Yesterday 68
Things I Believe 69
Phobic 70
Can't Find the Words 71
Where I Need To Be 72
See What You Did? 73

Dedicated to:

Sherice Brown
Ruth Robinson
Narecita Ibanez
Cathy Flake
Shannelle Cleckley
Stephanie H. Jameison (my big sis)
for their love and support

Daryl Simms
Troy Robinson
Christopher P. Fleming
who often served as poetic inspiration

and last but not least
Christopher X. Fleming
my wonderful ***sun***

www.ingramcontent.com/pod-product-compliance
Lightning Source LLC
Chambersburg PA
CBHW021024090426
42738CB00007B/895